Haiku 4 Justice
A 365+ Day Commentary of (In)Justice In America & Abroad

Poetry In the Age of Social Media

By
Discopoet
Khari B.
Discopoetry Publishing

I

Haiku 4 Justice
A 365+ Day Commentary on Social (In)Justice in America and Abroad
Poetry In the Age of Social Media
Copyright © 2019 by Khari B.

First printing: 2019
ISBN: 978-1-7335548-0-0
Discopoetry Publishing
Chicago, Illinois 60610

Edited by Dr. Tara Betts
Cover design by Khari B.
Direct ordering inquiries to info@disco-poetry.com
Appearance/performance requests to bookings@disco-poetry.com
Subject: Haiku 4 Justice

DEDICATION

2 the All.

2 the People.

2 my ancestors & spirits that watch over me: Thank U 4 leading me here.

2 my parents, Mwata and Judi Bowden who have been an unending source of support, love and education: Thank U.

2 my son: May U never B 2 comfortable 2 not work 4 your own betterment and that of the world around U. May U always B courageous enough 2 do that work.

2 my family: Your support and encouragement were necessary. Thank U 4 every bit of it.

2 my people, my elders, students, community, lovers & loved 1s: I hope I am doing U proud & using what U have given me. U have given me so much.

2 Philippe Gills, Cheryl Parks, Jasmine "Blondie" Morris, JLE & my Mama 2 being the largest contributors 2 making this book tangible: THANK U!

2 the fallen that inspired this book: I hope U hear us speak your name. Thank U 4 the work U R doing on the other side.

2 Uncle Bill, Big Rob, Baba Sam, Mama Ann, Linda, Linda, Tony, Juanita, Baba Kwesi, Renada, Tiffany, Shelton, Brenda & Mike: I miss U.

2 the beasts that inspired this book: U will pay.

IV

Contents

Haiku 4 Justice
A 365+ Day Commentary of (In)Justice In America & Abroad

Poetry In the Age of Social Media

Forward/Foreword
By jessica Care moore

ne year of a black life is difficult to explain in 3 lines, 17 syllables.
mehow, Khari B has eloquently achieved this task. Haiku 4 Jus-
e Poems are a tremendously poignant, and absolutely necessary col-
ction of Haiku from one of Chicago's longtime voices of poetry.

"4 Eric 2" the poet explains how black lives matter less than loose squares
d speeches. The read is a consistent punch of jabs at the white supremacist
nstruct of institutionalized racism. It also is a call to action to our own com-
unity to self reflect on issues of self-love, self- preservation and economic
npowerment. Getting free is the only ideology of these small, weighted
oems. These 3 lines poems are bombs, unapologetically lighting up the
age. Khari insists we must use what our ancestors left us, beneath our skin.

ike Haki Madhubuti's *Don't Cry, Scream*, published in 1969 Khari's poems
re screaming for justice, for the right to breathe in 2017 and beyond. The
ork resonates with the sound of resistance, a truth necessary for self worth
nd black empowerment. He challenges the power of simply praying without
oing the on-the-ground work to make change in one's city or global commu-
ity. His poems are always strapped, and he suggests the reader stays ready too.

n "G'Morning Brother and Sister" Khari asks black people to stop be-
ng afraid of their own people. He insists that this is not the year, the
ime or place for devaluing our worth. My personal favorite is #72.
'Only Revolution Can Stop This Pain" is the collective heartbreak of
o many women, and the life and death of Sandra Bland in a Texas jail.

I've Avoided U
Sandra. My heart can only
Break so many times.

These poems are painful, and they also celebrate. They honor the victory,
dominance and beauty of Serena and Venus Williams and the heart of
Muhammed Ali.

Khari B. is attempting to expose and find ways to heal the pain of being Bla
in America. To simply be human, is a task for families, for mothers, for
thers. While poems can't stop bombs, they can incite great action. *Haiku*
Justice is a platform for change; a daily remembrance; a cry for peace; a pray
for justice; a weapon against the failure of men to make this country the la
of the free.

Can we change the world in 17 syllables? Perhaps not. Still…

silence will kill us
leave us to die on our block
on a sunny day

jessica Care moor
Poet, Publisher, Moore Black Pre

4

Introduction

I began writing this on the train on the way 2 perform at Regina Badiocchi's "HaikuFest" 2015 N Chicago. She booked me as a guest performer 4 this annual event. I had prepared a number of pieces 2 share that day within the timespan allotted and was com4table with my planned presentation. Then it hit me, this was a festival built around the art of haiku and, though it wasn't necessary, I didn't have a single haiku in this present repertoire. I got 2 writing right then and there.

On that ride on Chicago's green line, I churned out 14 haiku not because I am (though I may be) some prolific writer but because without any major conscious thought or hesitation my chosen subject matter was the growing dissatisfaction over social justice issues largely stemming from the unpunished and unprovoked brutalization and many murders of unarmed men, woman and children raging across America at that very moment. How could I write about anything else?

I was pretty sure that the work wouldn't exactly B what was expected by an audience largely populated by European descendants but allowing the populace 2 live N ignorance or ignoring these issues goes against the calling of the artist. So selections from those 1st 14 haiku were worked N2 my show and warmly received by a large enough portion of the audience.

Afterward, I felt that I was on 2 something. Already I had been reflecting on how I should B writing more on a daily basis. Already I knew that I had not been doing enough of my part as an artist 2 directly address these issues of brutality, murder and injustice in this time. Already inside of me these poems were smoldering and I had not yet begun 2 write. The moment had presented itself and I accepted the challenge.

Haiku was something that we learned about briefly in 3rd grade. Short Japanese poems about nature that helped us creatively understand the nature of syllables. Nothing really exciting but a cool exercise 4 our expanding minds. They would come up again here and there along my educational matriculation through grade and high school and then it was done. In college I went N2 architectural engineering and haiku was officially a thing of the past. However, silently and rather unconsciously, I was still writing. Not haiku necessarily, but creative writing had become a private outlet aside from my academic studies and social life.

Years later, my mother, a creative in her own right, read about Richard Wright's profound feat of writing over 4000 haiku in 18 months. Retired and inspired, she decided 2 challenge herself 2 surpass Wright's output and got 2 producing new haiku almost daily at an amazing rate. Largely biblically informed, she wrote piece after piece per a schedule that she had set 4 herself and within a year's time she had not only beat Wright's record but that of her own as well. I was impressed.

Now I had no desire 2 attempt such a feat but her personal accomplishment inspired me 2 use this same platform 2 address this maddening matter of the murder of melanated people happening all over America. At the time, I had not even considered that this was a global issue but that fog would quickly clear as the stories would pour N.

I think initially I was writing with the thought 2 include the work in a friendly Facebook challenge between my friends 2 write 30 poems in 30 days but I couldn't stop. I don't know at what point I decided I would continue 4 a year but even then, I couldn't stop. The truth is the abject circumstances that institutional racism has propagated on this planet has infuriatingly given me more material 2 write about than I could ever cover. I wrote every one of these poems hoping that at some point I wouldn't have anything of this nature 2 write about. That never once happened. Every day there was a new murder or new assault by police, a new court decision that spit in the face of justice and that of the American public, a new atrocity backed by a U.S. politician or committed by the U.S. military or even somewhere else in the world where European conniving colonialism spread and festered. The acts, ALL rooted in the deeply entrenched racism in this world, has never paused. These sick men and infected mentalities never seem 2 run out of evils 2 inflict. So, I just kept writing so that there will always B a record from the People's point of view of how things went down in this time 4 a time when these conditions may no longer exist and the People need a reminder 2 stay ever vigilant as not 2 allow them 2 ever rise again.

This book is also filled with our hopes, our triumphs, our call 2 action. I write hoping that it will inspire the readers and those infected by them 2 act in a way 2 render these writings passé. I don't believe N much but I believe THAT will 1 day soon, within my lifetime, B true.

2 the critics and literary purists, that will undoubtedly come and read this work through eyes conditioned by false supremacist mentalities and say that these works do not fit the canon and tradition of haiku, I would remind U that I am the creator here. I am the artist and they do exactly what I want them 2 do in the framework that I have chosen. These poems R poems about nature; the nature of sick men, of murderers and savages in positions of widely accepted authority; of oppressed people and my reflections on how they react 2 their oppression; on the nature of resistance, defiance, clarity and hope. This is African-centered self-determination written through a Japanese tool. Though I usually write Blues-descended Rock (Chuck Berry/Little Richard) and Funk (James Brown/Parliament/Funkadelic) this is my Social music (Miles Davis) record, in book form, and I'm okay with that. In the tradition of my forebearers and ancestors, I've taken what exists and have made it my own.

Thank U 4 reading,
Khari B.

Note: U will find a number of "Ike" (ē-kay) scattered amongst these haiku. It's a form developed by Nigerian-American singer/poet Ugochi Nwaogwugwu written in 3 lines, syllabically based on a 3,5,8 pattern. The pattern takes its form from the number of letters in red (3), black (5), and green (8) as a reverent nod 2 the Pan-African flag of liberation and its creator, Marcus Garvey. Many respects 2 her 4 sharing this with me.

Timeline

4/19/15

#JusticeForFreddieGray – 25 year-old Freddie Gray dies from injuries 2 his spinal cord that occurred while being transported in a police van from an arrest a week earlier. Outside of claims of unreasonable force used in his arrest, officers failed 2 secure Gray properly N2 the transport vehicle where it is alleged that he sustained his injuries. 6 cops were brought up on charges on 2nd degree murder, depraved-heart murder, illegal imprisonment and more. No 1 was convicted. This incident began the inspiration 4 this series that I would begin writing 6 days later.

5/22/15

#ICantBreathe – I created a piece paralleling the U.S. corporations' wanton destruction of nature 2 the death of Eric Garner, who was murdered by a gang of cops from the Staten Island police department on July 17, 2014. Garner, who was approached after cops were called 4 an earlier fight, was targeted, known 4 selling loose cigarettes in the area. He was set upon by the gang who attempted 2 restrain and wrestle him 2 the ground as he resisted their unwarranted attack. The choke, that left strap muscle hemorrhages in his neck, came from 1 officer Pantaleo who callously ignored Garner's warnings that he couldn't breathe.

5/23/15

#Breloverdict – Cleveland officer Michael Brelo, one of 13 cops who shot 137 rounds of ammo N2 a car holding Timothy Russell and Malissa Williams, is found not-guilty. Both individuals were unarmed. Both of them were killed.

6/9/15

#WeAreDajerria – Responding 2 a call about a fight in a subdivision in suburban Dallas, McKinney police corporal Eric Casebolt tackles and slams a non-resistant 15 year-old Dajerria Becton. Becton, who was not involved in the incident 4 which the police were called, is drug by her hair and handcuffed with Casebolt sitting on her back with his knees and shoving her face N2 the grass. Becton weighed about 100lbs. Casebolt later refers 2 the group of children as a mob. Casebolt's attorney attributes his actions 2 Casebolt having a rough day. He resigned during the investigation but a grand jury declined 2 indict him.

6/12/15

Pink parents of 1 Rachel Dolezal confirms 4 police and the press that their little black-faced baby, who was working as a president of the NAACP, Spokane, Washington chapter at the time was in fact wholly of European descent. Bizarre details of the so-called transracial woman's life come 2 light including a claim of having been the victim of 9 hate crimes. Black Twitter has a field day that lasts 4 weeks immortalizing the hilarious hashtag #AskRachel.

6/17/15

#terrorism101 – 21-year old "white" supremacist, Dylann Roof, within the space of six minutes, murders nine members of the Emanuel African Methodist Episcopal Church in Charleston, SC. during their Wednesday night bible study with the hope of igniting a race war. Roof took part in the study session and prayed with the members B4 retrieving a .45 caliber Glock 41 and began shooting. The shooting came on the 193rd anniversary of Denmark Vesey's foiled uprising. Captured the following day 1 state over, Roof was treated 2 a Burger King meal by Shelby, NC police. At his hearing, survivors and relatives shared that they were "praying 4 his soul" and that they 4gave him.

6/27/15

#FreeBree – While lawmakers continued a never-ending debate regarding the history and "possible" racial impropriety of the Confederate flag within the South Carolina capitol, Bree Newsome, a 30 year-old filmmaker, songwriter and activist, scales a 30-foot flagpole 2 remove the battle flag right there on the capitol grounds. Addressing her action she said, "We removed the flag today because we can't wait any longer. We can't continue like this another day..." echoing the writings of Dr. Martin Luther King Jr. 51 years later. 2 weeks later the State voted 2 have it officially removed.

July 2015

#WhoIsBurningBlackChurches – Within 1 week of the Emanuel AME massacre by Dylann Roof, 5 predominately Black churches R set ablaze, echoing a trend of 145 of these churches burned between 1995 and 1996. More continued the following week. Though "authorities" R hesitant 2 label these intentional fires "Hate Crimes," the Bureau of Alcohol, Tobacco, Firearms and Explosives ruled 29 of the 79 fires that year 2 B by arson. Since 1996 the count was 2378 where 2/3rds of the time the perpetrator was Caucasian.

7/10/15

#SayHerName #SandySpeaks – Texas trooper Brian Encinia is fired behind perjury around his arrest of Chicagoan, Sandra Bland during a "routine traffic stop." An outspoken decrier of European supremacist pathology, Sandra was threatened by Encinia out of her car, manhandled and arrested during the altercation. 3 days later she is found dead hanging in her cell with a plastic garbage bag around her neck. Her death was ruled a suicide. Forensic investigators later find numerous inconsistencies in the official story including time of death and an unusual amount of THC in her blood stream.

7/11/15

#SerenaSlam – Serena Williams wins her 6th Wimbledon singles title defeating Spain's Garbine Muguruza, winning 4 straight major heats.

N commemoration of #BlackAugust

- August 2, 1924 – Author and social critic James Baldwin is born

- August 7, 1970 – 17 year old Johnathan Jackson is gunned down in his effort to liberate the Soledad Brothers with Black Liberation Fighters James McClain, William Christmas and Ruchell Magee outside of the Marin County California courthouse.

- August 14, 1791 – Dutty Boukman & Cécile Fatiman officiate the Vodou ceremony at Bois-Caiman to initiate and bless the Haitian Revolution which stands as the most successful rebellion of physically enslaved people in modern history.

- August 13, 1887 – the Honorable Marcus Mosiah Garvey is born.

- August 21, 1831 – Nat Turner launches an insurrection that would take the lives of 55-65 enslavers.

- August 21, 1850 – the Cazenovia Fugitive Slave Law Convention presided over by Frederick Douglass and attended by over 2000 people in protest of the impending Fugitive Slave Act.

- August 21, 1971 George Jackson of the Black Panther Party and co-founder of the Black Guerrilla Family is assassinated during a San Quentin prison rebellion.

- August 22, 1791 marks the Night of Fire" that ignited the Haitian Revolution.

- August 27, 1935 - Mary McLeod Bethune founds the National Council of Negro Women.

- August 28, 1888 - Granville T. Woods patents railway telegraphy.

- August 28, 1963 – The March on Washington for Jobs and Freedom pulls 2gether 250,000 people for the action.

- August 29, 1920 - Saxophonist Charlie "Bird" Parker is born.

- August 30, 1800 – B4 being betrayed by slaves 2 their masters, 24 year-old Gabriel organized what is said 2 B between several hundred to thousands of enslaved people 4 an insurrection in Virginia.

- August 30, 1948 Chairman Fred Hampton of the Black Panther Party for Self-Defense is born.

9/8/15

#tennisgirls – Serena Williams beats sister, Venus Williams in US Open quarter-final. It is her 11th win out of 16 against her high ranking champion sibling. Venus afterwards expresses 2 her younger sister. "I'm so happy 4 U." It is a beautiful moment in sports history.

9/30/15

#usualsuspects – The site "Blacks in Law Enforcement of America" reports a story of how off-duty Providence PD officer, Christopher Owens was brutally arrested helping to catch a fleeing suspect after the suspect and pursuing officers crashed N2 his front yard. After Owens and his son Tyler tackled the Caucasian suspect, they were punched in the face and handcuffed at the scene by officers Rawnsley, Furtado, Lt. Perez and State Detective McGarrity. Not only had Owens identified himself as an officer, he also alleges that he had worked shifts with the others N the past. The officers N question thought he was 1 of the perpetrators and 1 remarked "all we saw was a big black guy." Owens filed a civil suit against the department.

10/1/15
#4myson – 4 my bull-headed son to whom I hope this entire series inspires and expands.

10/17/15
#MatthewAjibade – Jury acquits Savannah, Georgia sheriff deputies Jason Kenny and Maxine Evans of the involuntary manslaughter of Matthew Ajibade, a bipolar sufferer who died N their custody, handcuffed 2 a chair, beaten and tased to death.

10/18/15
#thatbull – Chicago Mayor Rahm Emanuel blames Chicago's escalating murder rate on "the chilling effects of high-profile protests against police brutality and officers' fear of cell phone videos of their actions going viral." (~the Grio) FBI Director James Comey joined him in that sentiment later that month in a talk with students at the University of Chicago Law School.

#SomeoneTellKayihura #Ugandadecides – Human Rights Watch reports on Ugandan police attacking peaceful protesters around their upcoming elections using teargas, rubber bullets and physical brutality including an incident at the Main Street Primary School in Jinja.

#Justice4Corey – Drummer, Corey Jones, 31, is killed by Palm Beach Gardens police officer Nouman Raja, a cop with a history of disciplinary issues, while Jones was waiting on roadside assistance on Interstate 95. Jones' car had stopped traveling home after an evening gig. Raja was placed on paid administrative leave and later terminated from his job. Criminal charges weren't filed until June of the following year.

10/24/15
#FeesMustFall – Sparked by a tuition hike of up to 11.5%, protests, largely by students, continue across South Africa. They R met by police firing stun grenades, rubber bullets and teargas. President Jacob Zuma would eventually announce a 0% fee increase 4 2016 and on the 26th of October a memorandum was signed that conceded 13 of the students' demands temporarily ending the protest. Winnie Mandela publically voiced her support of the protests.

10/27/15
#AssaultAtSpringValleyHigh – Officer Ben Fields of the South Carolina sheriff's department is caught on video slamming a 16 year old girl 2 the ground B4 dragging her across the floor at Spring Valley High School N Columbia, SC. He was fired by the department 2 days later after the video went viral. Fields had already been sued twice for his misconduct as an officer. Superintendent Debbie Hamm went on record saying student safety is their #1 priority.

11/3/15
Between front-running GOP Candidate, Ben Carson's claims of Obama Care being "the worse thing that has happened in this nation since slavery", #AllLivesMatter & segregated bathrooms 4 transgendered people statements and Raven Symone's "I'm an American and that is a colorless person," "I was N that *culture*" [italics added] and her victim-blaming stance on #AssaultAtSpringValleyHigh this day's poem was born.

#JeremyMardis – Marksville, LA police brutally shoot and kill autistic 6 year-old Jeremy Mardis N the pursuit of the boy's father. Both individuals were unarmed, the father having his hands raised at the time. Both officers had pending suits against them for use of excessive force and 1 of them, Stafford, had previously been indicted on 2 counts of aggravated rape (2011). The 2 perpetrators surrendered themselves on 11/6/15 & were charged with 2nd degree murder and 2nd degree attempted murder due 2 the evidence captured on video by body cam. After bonding out, both murderers were placed on house arrest while awaiting trial, which, as of this publishing is in the spring and summer of 2017. All individuals involved were of European descent.

11/13/15

#MomsOnPatrol – Dedicated 2 the residents in and around 75th & Stewart where Mothers (& Men) Against Senseless Violence set up shop earlier that year 2 deter some of the violence that took the life Lucille Barnes (34) who was trying 2 break up a fight. M.A.S.K.'s direct action led 2 a drop in violent crime in the immediate area that very 1st summer. Their efforts continue.

11/19/15

The story of Fay Wells, a highly educated and well employed executive at a California company, who was confronted by 19 cops, some with guns drawn, who thought she had broken N2 her own home after receiving a call from her Caucasian neighbor is released in the press. Wells had locked herself out and had a professional lock service come 2 get her back N. Wells writes she is still traumatized from the event.

11/24/15

#JusticeforLaquan – Chicago Police Officer Jason Van Dyke was finally charged with the murder of Laquan McDonald that occurred the previous year, October 20, 2014. Van Dyke was charged with first-degree murder and held without bail at Cook County Jail but was later released on bail N November. This marked the 1st time a cop had received such a charge 4 such an action in almost 35 years. With evidence of an attempted cover-up, protests erupted 4 months demanding changes in police and judicial procedure and 4 the dismissal or resignation of both the mayor and State's Attorney (it didn't happen).

Dec. 2015

#bluelivesmatter - …represented a rash of not-guilty verdicts in numerous cases of police brutality and murder. The beating of unarmed Kyle Howell in Nassau County, NY, the murder of Freddie Gray N Baltimore, the murder of Laquan McDonald in Chicago and of 12 year old Tamir Rice N Cleveland. All of the perpetrators in all of those cases walked free for 1 reason or another.

Most often the murderers would claim they were afraid for their lives.

#JusticeforSandy – The man in charge of the jail where Sandra was held and found dead, Sheriff R. Glenn Smith, was put in charge of the Waller County's investigation of her death. Calls 4 an independent investigation were made. The FBI took the case. N December a grand jury abstained from issuing an indictment for Sandra Bland's death but the following January found the arresting officer, Brian Encinia guilty of perjury relating to his testimony. He was charged with a Class A misdemeanor. He paid a bond of $2,500 and was released after being arrested on that charge. Encinia was later fired as a state trooper.

Jan. 2016
#FlintWaterCrisis – Michigan Gov. Rick Snyder declares a state of emergency due 2 the lead content of Flint's drinking water. Less than 2 weeks later so does U.S. president Barack Obama, putting FEMA in charge of providing equipment and resources 2 the affected people. On Jan. 21 the Environmental Protection Agency determines that the City of Flint and the State of Michigan have inadequately responded to the water crisis and issues an order to take action. The issue originally began in April 2014 when Flint officials were searching 4 a cheaper water supply. No criminal charges R filed until April 12, 2015 and then later in July. After news breaks, people and organizations around the country begin 2 send truckloads of bottled water to Flint. As of this printing, Flint's water issues have not been corrected.

1/20/16
April Goggans, a DC-based BLM protester, interrupts the opening press conference at the United States Conference of Mayors in DC. Goggans stepped in front of the main podium quietly holding a sign that said, "16 shots and a cover up #LaquanMcDonald #ResignRahm" during an address by Baltimore Mayor Stephanie Rawlings-Blake. The moment was broadcast across national news sources.

2/3/16
#RosaLeeIngram #twitterstorians – The Atlanta Daily World reports on the impending death sentence of Rosa Lee Ingram and her 2 sons, Wallace and Sammie on Feb. 3, 1948. The Ingrams were sentenced 2 die 4 the

death of John Stratford, a tenant farmer who was said 2 have threatened Rosa Lee with a rifle that would end up being used 2 beat him 2 death by her 2 sons. Though claiming self-defense, the Ingrams were sentenced 2 die by an all Caucasian jury in Americus, GA. The Atlanta Daily World's coverage of the story brought national attention 2 the case and people of color from around the country, including celebrities like Lena Horne demanded justice 4 the Ingrams. Monies poured in 2 the ADW and the NAACP 2 assist Rosa Lee who had 12 children total. The judge granted a stay of execution. It would B 11 years B4 they were all released.

2/4/16
#blkhistoryfacts – On this day in 1986 19th century abolitionist and women's rights activist Sojourner Truth's likeness was placed on a U.S. stamp as a part of the U.S. Postal Service's Black Heritage series.

2/7/16
#slay – Superbowl 50. California. Beyoncé. #Formation. Black Panther-ish. Yay.

2/19/16
#daywithoutlatinos #WisconsinisnotArizona– 14,000 people gather at the Wisconsin state capitol building in protest of 2 bills directed directly at targeting Latino and immigrant rights. Chicago Black Lives Matter leader, Aislinn Pulley declines a meeting at the White House writing in an op-ed 4 Truthout, "I could not, with any integrity, participate in such a sham that would only serve to legitimize the false narrative that the government is working to end police brutality and the institutional racism that fuels it." U.S. Congressmen call up U.S. Attorney General Loretta Lynch 2 investigate an alleged conspiracy between oil conglomerates regarding climate change while California official claim that the worst natural gas leak in U.S. history is finally capped after near 4 months. At its peak the leak sprayed the equivalent pollution of 4.5 million cars per day.

2/21/16
#MalcolmX – On this day in 1965, "our shining Black prince" el-Hajj Malik el-Shabazz aka Malcolm X was murdered in front of his family during a talk with the People at New York's Audubon Ballroom under a still suspicious and undisclosed conspiracy.

3/10/16

It's Harriet Tubman Day! In 1990 in recognition of this powerful warrior, abolitionist and humanitarian, the 101st U.S. Congress in conjunction with U.S. president George H. W. Bush declared this day as #HarriettTubmanDay. Tubman was born in Dorchester County, MD sometime in 1820. In an exemplary and remarkable life she freed herself from enslavement, freed hundreds of others, fought as a spy and soldier in the Civil War, spoke out against the institution of slavery, spoke up about women's suffrage and established a rest home 4 elderly Blacks among other things. She passed on this day N 1913.

3/16/16

#whoyoucallinganigga – Aleeyah Porter of Oklahoma was reportedly harassed by a young Caucasian associate who threatened 2 "blow her head off." Porter claimed 2 have told certain adults about the issue but it went unaddressed so Aleeyah went 2 C the girl herself on this day. In the videoed confrontation, the girl called Aleeyah a nigger. Aleeyah responded with a graceful right cross and proceeded 2 insure the girl never 4got the error of her ways. The video of young Aleeyah punching her way N2 Black History & N2 our hearts went viral with praises and curses coming from all directions while making material for the funniest memes EVER.

3/19/16

The Associated Press reports that the city of Chicago has dolled out $662 million in police misconduct settlements since 2004. In a span between March 2011 and Sept. 2015, out of the 28,500 citizen complaints filed against Chicago's police officers less than 2% resulted in discipline though the police union claims that in that same time misconduct "led to 45 firings and 28 suspensions." Chicago often claims 2 B a city without adequate funds 4 education, homelessness and other basic responsibilities of any tax-collecting municipality.

4/8/16

#Sprinter – While "He Who Shall Not Be Named" aka "the Cheeto" claimed global warming did not exist, Chicago and other places in the midwest and east coast of the U.S. were experiencing a snow storm when it should have been Spring.

4/15/16

Mass media reports that shootings in Chicago, the U.S.'s 3rd largest city yet ranked below the top 10 cities in murders, are up more than 88% and murders up 72%. This comes after the ACLU (American Civil Liberties Union) calls for police agencies to record all of their street stops for disproportionately targeting people of color 4 searches and questioning paralleling New York's "stop & frisk" issues. The departments points to the access to guns by "thugs." The People point at departments 4 supplying them such as in the May 9, 2014 case when ABC 7 news reported on 13 brand new assault rifles being stolen from a freight train sitting unsecured in Chicago's notorious Englewood area.

4/21/16

#Controversy – Music legend Prince Rogers Nelson dies of a supposed opioid overdose at his home, Paisley Park, in Chanhassen MN. On tour days prior, Prince had 2 have an emergency landing in Moline, IL outside of Chicago 4 what was reported as flu symptoms only 2 leave less than 24 hours later. Back 2 his usual business in the following days Prince was found dead at his estate in an elevator that he was said 2 never use. Initial reports did not state a cause of death. Later it was claimed 2 B a painkiller that Prince was known 2 have used due 2 hip surgery years B4. His body was cremated 2 days later and legal access was granted N2 the raiding of the Artist's famed vault. Beyond his music Prince was widely known 4 his public shunning of the music industry, championing of artist independence and 4 quietly funding non-profits in technology & Black Lives Matter campaigns.

4/27/16

#whatjustice – Dennis Hasert, former U.S. Speaker of the House, is sentenced 2 15 months in federal prison & 2 years of court supervision after release on a bank fraud case that centered around him being a serial child molester. A second banking charge that carried a 5-year sentence was dismissed. Hasert admitted 2 "mistreatment" of the boys during his time as a high school wrestling coach in Illinois. A statute of limitations supposedly prevented him from being charged with the molestation issue.

5/14/16

#whywomendontreport – On 2/14/16 a young woman of color studying overseas N Spain was drugged, taken and raped by a club promoter after a night of hanging out. Devastated, foggy and hurt she escaped and retreated back the home where she staying simply wanting 2 hide. Upon her friend's insistence, she went 2 the hospital 4 her injuries and 2 report the crime. There she was denied a rape kit, called a prostitute and had 2 fight 2 simply have a policeman take her report. In the days and weeks 2 follow she found little help from the U.S. Embassy, was essentially blamed 4 her assault by both the police department and the courts and had 2 endure C'ing her assaulter without being able 2 have him arrested. Resiliently, she successfully continued her studies 2 the end of the semester after which she returned home. Months later she was informed her case had been dropped.

There were no news reports, no rallies, not even any support groups made available 2 her. There were even a rash of women who were a part of the denial, degradation and disgusting behavior of those who would not consider the young lady's plight. She endured anyway.

2 many of our women go unprotected in these types of cases and 1 can venture that the unsympathetic treatment of an entire system that 2 often fails 2 give these and any women the support and justice they R entitled 2 can and does make matters far worse. We must do better.

5/19/16
#MalcolmX – Our shining prince, brotha Malcolm X, was born in Omaha Nebraska in 1925 2 Earl and Louise Little.

5/30/16
#memorialday – The 1st Memorial Day, held in 1865 by approximately 10,000 formally enslaved men and women N South Carolina, was in honor of the 54th Massachusetts & the 34th & 104th U.S. Colored Troop who fought in America's 1st Civil War.

6/3/16
#rememberJune3rd #PrayforGhana – More than 150 people lose their lives in Ghana during a fire at a fuel station which broke out during a flood in 2015. People had gathered at the station 4 shelter during a heavy downpour. A fire was lit from oil float-

ing on top of the water from a suspected cigarette butt. A year and 1 week after, more flooding claims the lives of another 10. Western media does little reporting of these international tragedies.

6/4/16
#thegreatestofalltime #Ali – Muhammad Ali, powerful pugilist, humanitarian and controversial revolutionary human rights activist 4 people of color passes at the age of 74.

6/13/16
#MichaelMoore – 19-year old Michael Moore was murdered by officer Harry Hurst in Mobile, AL during what was called a routine traffic stop. Mike and 3 other people were pulled over after an alleged traffic violation where he was found not 2 have a driver license on him. Hurst ordered Mike out of the car whereupon he claimed to have seen Mike reach 4 a gun in his waistband. Mike was shot at least 4 times, 3 of those shots after he had fallen. Conflicting reports state that the gun was only retrieved after Moore had been taken 2 the hospital, dismissed as "a mistake in protocol" by the police chief. Witnesses state that Hurst shot Mike with his hands in the air within seconds of ordering him 2 the ground. Alabama is an open carry state.

7/18/16
#Idontknow – SWAT team member Jonathan Aledda fires 3 shots from a rifle, shooting 47 year old Charles Kinsey in his leg while Kinsey laid on the ground, hands raised, after attempting to retrieve an autistic patient that was in his care. Kinsey is handcuffed after the shooting and left bleeding in the street for roughly 20 minutes. SWAT was supposedly responding 2 a call about a man threatening 2 shoot himself. When Kinsey, who survived the shooting, asked Aledda Y he shot him Aledda famously answered, "I don't know."

8/1/16
#KorrynGaines #SayHerName – Baltimore County Police murder 23 year old Korryn Gaines in their alleged attempt 2 issue a bench warrant 4 failure 2 appear in court regarding an alleged traffic violation. Asserting her rights and the unlawfulness of the police's actions, Korryn refused and closed herself off in her home with her son, wielding a shot-

gun for protection. The hours long standoff was marked by the lack of body camera footage from the police directly involved, though those in supporting roles wore them. Korryn herself streamed what was happening via Facebook until police had her account shutdown with a request to Facebook. This move by the multi-billion dollar company lead 2 much criticism regarding their action as a threat 2 civil liberties. After her social media feed was shut down, police raided her home, shot her 2 death and shot her 5 year old son in the arm. Korryn never fired a shot. No criminal charges were filed & the shooting was deemed justified.

Protests erupted after her murder while the City of Baltimore and the police department attempted to assassinate her character by claiming she used her child as a shield during the incident and by referring to her as mentally deficient for identifying herself as a "free person" refusing 2 accept their assumed authority. This technique was similar 2 how slave owners claimed that enslaved people that ran away from their enslavement suffered from a mental condition that they would call drapetomania.

As usual, the media found numerous people of color who would support the "official" claims of a mental disability and condemn her actions N the press. News of any possible validity 2 Korryn's claims of being a "free person" and the lawfulness of her actions were never explored or investigated by the popular press.

April 2015

Hate vs Fear
Our lives do matter
Your hate of us matters not
It's your fear that kills
4/29/15 (*4/25/15*)

Dress Code
Deadly fashions change
White hoods went out of style
Now they wear badges
4/30/15 (*4/25/15*)

May 2015

Expediency
Innocent until
proven guilty was once law
Trigger pulls save time
5/1/15 (*4/25/15*)

The Outrage
Murdered boys & girls
R not an epidemic
unless they're pink-skinned
5/4/15 (*4/25/15*)

Cowards
Brown-skinned boys & girls
definitely pose a threat
They expose your fear
5/5/15 (*4/25/15*)

Cultural Appropriation
Y would I have to
explain Y our lives matter
U steal all we do
5/6/15 (*4/25/15*)

Proper Defense
When a cop is killed
I hope the shooter will say
I feared for my life
5/7/15 (*4/25/15*)

I Can't Hear U
Your profound silence
is far louder than your words
It shows your concern
5/8/15 (*4/25/15*)

Relativity
Our Black lives matter
Not over anyone else
Not under either
5/11/15 (*4/25/15*)

U Matter
Our Black lives matter
4 all the beauty we share
4 all that we do
5/12/15 (*4/25/15*)

Genesis
In the beginning
there was only us – darkness
We gave birth 2 light
5/13/15 (*4/25/15*)

Ra(y)
Children of the Sun
continue 2 shine brightly
Hate can't dim our glow
5/14/15 (*4/25/15*)

Reflection
It is our beauty
that mirrors the Sun above
All God's children do
5/15/15 (*4/25/15*)

Some of Y'all R Confused
War has been declared
Only one side is engaged
Call it genocide
5/18/15 (*4/25/15*)

Patience Is Not A Virtue
Old age has taken
many waiting 4 justice
from the status quo
5/19/15 (*4/25/15*)

Exceptions
Everybody wants
a bloodless revolution
Your blood's okay though
5/20/15 (*4/25/15*)

Gun Control
Begging 4 justice
from the unjust hasn't worked
Hands down – Hold it tight
5/21/15

4 Eric
I can't breathe means naught
They were destroying the air
long B4 Garner
5/22/15

U've Been Given Your Instructions
Hands out of the air
Protect yourself at all times
U're still a target
5/25/15

4 Eric 2
Things that matter more
than Black lives: pink skin, loose squares
speeches, bottom lines
5/26/15

Indoctrination
　　Our lives pale under
　　their pale skin and privilege
　　The lie we accept
　　5/27/15

Prioritization
　　Love us like U love
　　designer names and gossip
　　& we can't B stopped
　　5/28/15

What Does Self-Love Look Like
　　If we loved ourselves
　　like we've been taught to love them
　　we'd B free right now
　　5/29/15

Intersectionality
Let's get free, brotha
& sista is the only
ideology
5/30/15

We's Sick, Boss?
When they self-destruct
which they most certainly will
some of U go 2
5/31/15

June 2015

No More Questions
U R the answer
End asking those who hate U
2 save yo Black ass
6/1/15

Genesis 1:26
Dependency is
not attractive. Time 2 build
N your own image
6/2/15

Indoctrination 2
U pledged your alle-
giance 2 a thief B4 know-
ing your own genius
6/3/15

The Unity Answer
We ain't got 2 a-
gree 2 ride out 2gether
4 our own people
6/4/15

While U Were Out Marching
Did U C them laugh-
ing behind your mad backs when
they passed that verdict?
6/5/15

U Look Stupid
The joke has always
been on U. Why R U at
the table laughing?
6/6/15

2 n 1
They will never re-
spect U (but they do adore/fear
U enough 2 steal/kill
6/7/15

While U've Got Your Hands Up
They Rn't interested
N taking U alive, Black
Non-violence 4 what?
6/8/15

We Prescribe
When U C small girls
as monsters 2 B conquered
U should kill yoself
6/9/15

& Y'all Wonder Y
Pool parties R not
hunting grounds, U demon pig
Well, they shouldn't B
6/10/15

Party Poopers Always Got 2 Ruin Sh**
Pool parties were not
hunting grounds, U filthy pigs
until U showed up
6/11/15

Fry 'Em
Pork fries up crispy
N a skillet & a chair
Officer Bacon
6/12/15

Job Qualifications
Hidden cowardice
Celebrated savagery
Just part of the job
6/13/15

Recompense
They let U resign
Cowardice should not B paid
or have a pension
6/14/15

At the Root
Scared of being left out
they ain't really interested
N diversity
6/15/15

Escape Clause
Pink girl in blackface
can switch back when it goes bad
Her defenders can't
#AskRachel 6/16/15

#AskRachel

New Tricks
Pink girl N blackface
used cloaking device 2 steal
instead of a pen
6/17/15

Coon Squad
Pink girl N blackface
got your job and scholarship
U defending her?
6/18/15

Trust
Can't B here 4 U
Like U claimed 2 B 4 us
Your life is a lie
6/19/15

When U Really Break It Down
She really tried
Empathy isn't blackface
Her ass just crazy
6/20/15

Things Passed Down From Our Ancestors
2 know the struggle
1 must use more than just eyes
It's beneath the skin
6/21/15

The Domino Effect
Don't understand Y?
Cops have shown U can B killed
without consequence
6/22/15

Traitorous Pacification
Everyone that says
"Let us kneel & pray 4 peace"
is your enemy
6/23/15

My Bible & My 45
Prayer don't stop bullets
& don't protect us from them
Pray, then lock and load
#Dylannroof #terrorism101 6/24/15

#Dylannroof #terrorism101

When the Mainline is Busy
Don't nobody die
like ni**as praying 2 B
saved – He ain't coming
6/25/15

Religious Conditioning
If U R waiting
still, 4 a savior 2 come
U can't C mirrors
6/26/15

Willful Blindness
Ain't knocking your God
Knocking U ignoring "His"
signs N front of U
6/27/15

By Necessity

We can't win by arms
alone – They've got more of them
Organize or die
6/28/15

By Necessity 2

We can't win by votes
They bought those a while ago
Organize or die
6/29/15

Impotence

U R prey 2 them
Lions eaten by locust
No roar – No respect
6/30/15

July 2015

Impotence 2
Your actions Rn't loud
despite your supposed outrage
Consumed by silence
7/1/15

4 Denise, Cynthia, Carol and Addie Mae
Yo church is burning
While U're busy 4giving
they're lighting 1 mo'
7/2/15

James 2:20
Burnt church folk
Please get up offa yo knees and
make them feel the heat
7/3/15
#ikes4justice

Whose Broad Stripes and Bright Stars?
How do U
celebrate your own slavery
Freedom's a-ways off
7/4/15
#ikes4justice

Rock the Vote?
Cast off illusions
of our inclusivity
It's pacifying
7/5/15

Assess the Beast
Take away all guns
BELIEVE, they will still kill U
Keep your hand on yours
7/6/15

The Sleeping Giant
Better get us now
while we're still on that bullsh**
We R waking fast
7/7/15

Don't Make Him A Liar
He thought we were tak-
ing over the country. So
Y the f*** R'nt we
7/8/15

Readjust Your Strategy
How's your vote working?
Politicians use U while
they empower hate
7/9/15

Readjust Your Strategy (prologue)
They give authority
2 murderers 2 kill U
as part of the job
7/10/15

No Confusion
It's not guns
that R massacring our folk
It's use by devils
7/11/15
#ikes4justice

G'morning Brotha/Sista
They've made U afraid
2 B with your own people
Take back your power
7/14/15

4 the Williams Sisters pt.1
Fu** them, Serena
Racism was in their eyes
blinded by your shine
7/15/15

4 the Williams Sisters pt.2
There is beauty in
your skin despite what they say
B bold with your being
7/16/15

4 the Williams Sisters pt.3
Hollywood wrote Wim-
bledon because they couldn't
beat U N real life
7/17/15

Priorities
More concern about
a flag than Sandra Bland's death
F*** wrong wit'chall folk?
#JusticeforSandy 7/18/15

Only Revolution Can Stop This Pain
I've avoided U
Sandra. My heart can only
break so many times
#JusticeforSandy 7/19/15

Empty Emotions
We let them take San-
dra, our women, our children
Standing around mad
#JusticeforSandy 7/20/15

Fall 1990
Not afraid 2 stand
Scared I'll B standing alone
Been shown enough times
7/21/15

Existential Singularity
U R being murdered
because U still haven't seen
it's U being murdered
7/22/15

Nothing 2 Lose
What's 2 B scared of?
U've seen they'll kill U any-
way. Resist or die
7/23/15

Frozen Warriors
I don't think we're cow-
ards. I think we've had the fight
beat up out of us
7/24/15

Uncle Willie's Phenomenon Shift
I think we 4got
how 2 fight anyone but
ourselves. Time 2 change
#fukisyalldoin 7/25/15

They Can't B 4 Real
I can't understand
how U're so quick 2 defend
them when they'll kill U
7/26/15
#causeIreallydontunderstand

New Port
Smoking is a su-
icidal act – like being
"Black" in the U.S.
7/27/15

Reciprocity
Until they feel what
we feel, this BS is going
2 keep happening
7/28/15

Public Service Announcement
Just in case, please know
I will NEVER kill myself
while in custody
7/29/15
#JusticeforSandy

How Unstoppable We Can B
If U join with me
personal beliefs aside
nothing can stop us
7/30/15

The Meek Shall Inherit The Ass Whuppin'
Don't U B quiet
Your people need 2 hear U
Been silent 2 long
7/31/15

August 2015
#BlackAugust

Clarity
We R not at war
In war, U don't stand by si-
lently getting killed
8/1/15

Priorities 2
It's not my concern
Keep the muthafu**in' flag
Change that damn mental
8/2/15

4 Denmark
Some have that "We's sick,
boss?" mentality real bad
Burn the house & slaves
8/3/15
#4Denmark

House Cleaning *(4 #GabrielProsser)*
The coons must go first
when it finally goes down
They'll ruin it all
8/4/15

House Cleaning 2 *(4 #BabaNat)*
They love massa 2
much 2 let him go alone
Let them pave the way
8/5/15

Uncle Iceberg Sam v. Yo Good Sense
They want 2 keep U
dependent like naïve whores
Walk the hell away
8/6/15

The Good Ol' Days?

(4 Mumia, Assata & all the brothas & sistas persecuted by the U.S. "Justice" system)

Remember when the
justice system was just? Me
neither. Could B though
8/7/15

Y I've Been Writing This *(4 #BabaGarvey)*

Every word I write
is 2 inspire U &
me 2 do better
8/8/15

C Ya! *(4 Shine the stoker)*

Shine knew when 2 bail
Left pinky on their sinking
ship – Get the message?
8/9/15

No Negotiation – No Prisoners
Bye, Miss Laura
Ancestor of Shaft
Django understood warfare
Tell Miss Laura Bye
8/10/15
#Djangosrevenge

Just My Type *(4 #PamGrier)*
All 4 yo people
& damn fine at the same time
Thanks, Sheba Baby
8/11/15

Who R U Working 4? *(4 the #Workers)*
Don't use Ogun's ham-
mer 4 the wrong people John
Henry. Pound 4 us
8/12/15

Y U Leave Him With Me, Easy?
(4 #DonCheadle)
Mouse knew what 2 do
When it comes down 2 it, I'll
leave them with him 2
8/13/15

She Sees *(4 #TheOracle)*
Mama, we need your
sight. Your vision is clearer
& U know the way
8/14/15

How 2 Use Your Resources
(4 Baba #SamGreenlee)
Dan's a bad mutha
Turned gangstas N2 soldiers
when the war was on
8/15/15

4 The Love of Hip-Hop 0/Revisionism *(4 #PE)*
Those Niggas 4 Life
weren't a public enemy
More like the feds' pets
#realhiphop 8/16/15

4 The Love of Hip-Hop 1
(4 #KendrickLamar)
We GO'N B alright
Thank U 4 the reminder
That's putting N work
#realhiphop 8/17/15

4 The Love of Hip-Hop 2
(4 #SaRoc & #MCLyte)
A modern-day light
from a long line of ladies
who make word divine
#realhiphop 8/18/15

4 The Love of Hip-Hop 3
(4 #JCole)
The brotha's got balls
2 share light in an indus-
try that castrates boys
#realhiphop 8/19/15

4 The Love of Hip-Hop 4
(4 #LaurynHill)
U shared hope while
U sang through evident pain
Heard Goddess through U
#realhiphop 8/20/15

4 The Love of Hip-Hop 5
(4 #X-Clan)
"This is protected..."
The wake up call we needed
The pride we deserve
#realhiphop 8/21/15

4 The Love of Hip-Hop 6
(4 #KRS-1)
No better show or
message consistently dropped
from any MC
#realhiphop 8/22/15

While U're Busy Asking/Begging, 378 Years Ago…
(4 #Yanga)
Primer Libertador
de America, Nyanga
MADE them respect us
8/23/15

Concessions
(4 #theMaroons)
Osceola and
Toussaint. Captured the same way
Lies. We can't trust them
8/24/15

Make Them Respect U
(4 the #Seminoles)
John Horse let 'em know
We make war. Not slave revolts
We're enslaved. Not slaves
8/25/15

Edict *(4 #DuttyBoukman)*
Call on our ances-
tors. Cast off their gods. Burn it
all. In that order
8/26/15

Never 4get What We're Fighting 4
(4 #Dessalines)
When the war is won
and our foe vanquished, respect
OUR needs above all
8/27/15

In the Face of Thine Enemies
(4 #Emmett)
Till wasn't killed 4
a whistle. It's because he
had no fear of them
8/28/15

Do Not Tire
(4 our ancestors)
There R those who did
a lot more with a lot less
4 a lot longer.
8/31/15
#justgettingstarted

September 2015

Message Received
I don't need 2 C
another victim 2 know
these beasts must B stopped
9/1/15

Some of Y'all R F***ed Up In the Head
Waiting 4 justice
from the unjust is an act
of insanity
9/2/15

The Assist
It's not so bad U're
inactive. It's that U help
them slide it in us
9/3/15
#blackbadges #blueline

Black Pig's On the Menu 2
Beware shedding your
uniform, brotha in blue
They won't exclude U
9/4/15
#blackbadges #blueline

Only 1 Choice
We're going 2 need U
Hopefully U'll hold your peo-
ple over your job
9/5/15
#blackbadges #blueline

It's Just Protocol
They'll use your genius
your might, your skills then turn a-
round & don't know U
9/6/15
#theindoctrinated

It's Just Protocol 2
They'll use your genius
your might, your skills until there
is none left 4 U
9/7/15
#theindoctrinated

It's Been Protocol 4 1000s of Years
They'll use your genius
your might, your skills then pretend
U did not exist
9/8/15
#theindoctrinated

4 the Win *(4 Venus and Serena)*
Who won? They both did
Fam'ly is not competi-
tion. Adjust your sight
9/9/15

Birthing Suspects
We R born fitting
the description and indict-
ed 4 existing
9/10/15

May This Call B Finite
I don't want these poems
2 B timeless. Its aim is
2 B obsolete
9/11/15

The Gaddamn Nerve
U expect us 2
4get your atrocities
but recall your pains
9/11/15

Corporate Niggas *(4 #BobJohnson)*
True slaves with money
only reinvest back N
2 the plantation
9/12/15

The History Channel
When they say they don't
know where it came from it prob-
ably came from U
9/13/15

He Might've Gotten Ink On Me!
(4 Nehad)
The pen is not migh-
tier than the sword when the
sword fires bullets
9/14/15

So Y'd They Run?
Not running because
of guilt. We R literal-
ly scared 4 our lives
9/15/15

Appropriated Confusion
How U gonna B
mad at pink folks with fros &
locs but got a perm?
9/21/15
#assimilation

U Really Ain't Ready
How U gon' fight foes
on the outside when U can't
handle the inside?
9/22/15
#cleanupyoownbackyardfirst

The Delusion
(4 the brothas AND the sistas)
Sexist revolu-
tion ain't revolution at
all. Still ain't ready
9/23/15

I Bet U Think This Poem Is About U
Revolution is
not your ego-based indi-
vidualism
9/24/15
#getyospiritrightfirst

Maybe We SHOULD Assimilate & Act Like U
If we were more like
U, U'd hate us more. Not like-
ly U'd exist though
9/25/15
#notaminority #assimilation #genocidists

It's Only A Matter of Time
We think N abstracts
'til out faces hit concrete
Don't wait 'til it's U
9/26/15

Damned If U Don't
Sticking up 4 yours
does have its consequences
So does doing zilch
9/28/15

Silence The Noise
The beat of war drums
R lost beneath media
programmed confusion
9/29/15

Get Louder – The 90% Share
The sound of our drums
have been drowned out by 6 LOUD
sources of static
9/30/15

October 2015

Persistence
They may not hear us
NOW but we can't stop drumming
They will soon enough
10/1/15
#4myson

Toxic Tolerance
We hate ourselves e-
nough 2 put up with their bull
sh** 4 all these years
10/2/15

Bloody Concrete Evidence
Wanna know where 4-
giveness has gotten us? Ask
the next 1 murdered
10/3/15

U Were Warned
America passed
on a bloodless revolu-
tion. Remember that
10/4/15
#4Malcolm

Marching Orders
America passed
on bloodless revolution
Give em what they want
10/5/15
#4Malcolm

4 Our Next Trick
Gentrification
displaces those who're alrea-
dy disenfranchised
10/6/15

As We Run Out Of Space To Run
Gentrification
moves the marginalized but
not 4 much longer
10/7/15

The Encore
Gentrification
is 2day's localized co-
lonialism
10/8/15

Giving Them What U Got 2 Get What U Have
Integration is
devaluing your own wealth
N favor of theirs
10/9/15

When The Grass Ain't Greener
Integration is
devaluing what U have
2 live next 2 them
10/10/15

What Was Inside Us All The Time
They rely on us
4 economic support
Direct it within
10/11/15

Money, Money, Money, Mon-nay –MonnnNay
We could shut this down
NOW but our addiction 2
what they have is strong
10/12/15

Bigger Than Dollars
My prayer is that soon
we C our collective wealth
as the tool it is
10/13/15

Vagrants
We owned the land long
B4 they even got here
Time 2 get our rent
10/14/15
#RentNotReparations

Everything "White" Ain't Right
Let go of the il
lusion of their righteousness
& we'll B alright
10/15/15

Who's Doin' Who?
Making laws 2 make
being U criminal is
a crime N itself
10/16/15
#thenewjimcrow

#JusticeforCorey

Sorry Not Sorry/Keep Your Phony Apology
Cowards will say what
they have 2 N order not
2 pay 4 their crimes
10/17/15

Listen *(4 #CoreyJones)*
May we hear the sounds
of your drums beating from there
now Corey Jones. Damn
10/18/15

Keep Playing, Corey (*4 #CoreyJones*)
2 kill a musi-
cian is 2 try 2 kill the
voice of the People
10/19/15

#*JusticeforCorey*

Not Just Oranges
Florida murders
men of color with a cer-
tain impunity
10/20/15

Just Another Day On the Hunt
Untrained, dressed plain badge-
less & armed with an excuse
4 racial murders
10/21/15

& I Mean Every Word Of It
May U & the sys-
tem that supports U burn N
hell, Nouman Raja
10/22/15

So the Perp Is Known But Is Still Walking Free
May U rot N hell,
Nouman Raja, U racist
trigger-happy swine
10/23/15

#InjuryToOneInjuryToAll

In Solidarity
We often miss the
kinship of our resistance
Rise Azania
10/24/15
#feesmustfall

Pink Privilege
The fact we got 2
tell U that Black lives matter
shows there's a problem
10/25/15

We C Your Bullsh**
All lives matter did
not matter until we had
2 say Black lives did
10/26/15

4 our daughter at Spring Valley High

Safety: Our #1 Priority
Superintendent
Debbie Hamm, slamming students
does not make them safe
10/27/15

Our Daughter
If it were your lit-
tle girl would U want that pig
2 go on breathing?
10/28/15

Does She Not Deserve Retribution?
If it were your lit-
tle girl would U accept that
pig's apology?
10/29/15

4 our daughter at Spring Valley High

Empty Empathy
She'd already lost
so much when he decided
2 take her safety
10/30/15
#4BaconBenFields

Infected
What demon exists
N your soul that U would at-
tack a girl like that?
10/31/15
#4BaconBenFields

November 2015

The Snooze Button Blues
Waking up this sleep-
ing giant is costing 2
many lives. Wake up!
11/1/15

**The Snooze Button Blues: Just A Few More
Moments, Please**
Shots ring out loud. U
hear them crack almost daily
Wake up already!
11/2/15

They Always Find One
(*4 Ben Carson & Raven Symone*)
Justifying their
massas' savagery is what
these negroes do best
11/3/15

Not Never
(*4 Common. A reminder*)
Treating a savage
kindly has NEVER made them
any less savage
11/4/15

Peace Didn't Get King Less Murdered
Despite their differen-
ces both King & Malcolm were
murdered the same way
11/5/15

Did They Think They Were Exempt?
(*4 Jeremy Mardis*)
Systematically
all hell breaks loose now that they've
killed a young pink boy
11/6/15
#InjuryToOneIsInjuryAll

Let's Stop Pretending
Please stop asking 4
answers. Seek retribution
They don't give a fu**
11/7/15

Luke 6:29
How many cheeks do
U have left 2 turn brotha/sista?
That working 4 U?
11/8/15

2 Clear Any Confusion
Haikus R used 2
write about nature. I write
on that of this world's
11/9/15

4 Their Own Good
I'm trying not 2
hold this anger & pain so
I write these haiku
11/10/15

Warranted Indignation
It's difficult 4
me 2 use sweet words against
a rotted system
11/11/15

Sad Masochism
Y do we have trust
4 a justice system that's
been unjust 2 us?
11/12/15

Part of the Trap (*4 the block*)
Relegated 2
short-term decisions, it's hard
2 make long-term goals
11/13/15

Enough Tears Already
2 many mourning
when they should B avenging
How else will it stop?
11/14/15

The Magician's Assistant
Trained pigs do tricks like
tickets & maintain more crimes
than they ever stop
11/15/15

#ikes4justice

The Art of Distraction
We can miss
the farmer's guilt dis-
tracted by the pig's behavior
11/16/15

Within Department Protocol
There is no
justification
4 their acts of barbarity
11/17/15

They Don't C U (*4 Fay Wells*)
Maybe it's
our light that blinds them
& illuminates their envy
11/18/15

The Painful Realization (*4 Fay Wells*)
Degrees, nice
clothes & "safe" resi-
dences don't make U bulletproof
11/19/15

No Camouflage
Away with the myth
middle class disguises makes
U less threatening
11/20/15

Optimism
I'm pretty sure we
have the power 2 change what's
wrong with this system
11/21/15

Pessimism
I'm pretty sure it's
only fear that prevents us
from making that change
11/22/15

In 2day's News
Media is the
tool used 2 manufacture
the fear that grips us
11/23/15

When U Let Them Tell U Who U R
Tutsi, Hutu, Hai-
tian, Dominican, light skin
dark skin, hell born lies
11/24/15

There Shouldn't B A Reason 2 Write This
Seventeen syllables
4 sixteen shots. I don't
want 2 write this poem
11/25/15
4 #LaquanMcDonald

Reassess
We marched 4 Sandra
Eric, Mike Brown, Trayvon
It is not working
11/26/15
#justiceforLaquan

Reassess 2
We marched 4 Laquan
Aiyana & Corey Jones
They don't give a fu**
11/27/15

Band-Aids On Bullet Wounds
It isn't Justice
VanDyke is served up as a sacrifice
2 release some pressure
Boil over anyway
11/28/15
#notquiteahaiku

The Call 2 Arms Is Sounding
Love 2 y'all fighting
2 many folks just talking
Workers needed now
11/29/15

One Nation???
Nothing united
about these states except the
state of oppression
11/30/15

December 2015

...With Liberty & Justice 4???
These united states
that state people R free, free-
ly kill free people
12/1/15

Tolerance
Our oppression is
directly proportional
2 what we do take
12/2/15

Curable Insanity
This is no longer
endurance. It is madness
only we can end
12/3/15

Undeniable
This beauty of ours
is indomitable when
it's used together
12/4/15

The Necessity of Unity
Comprehend the pow-
er N our connections. There
is nothing stronger
12/5/15

Blocked Traffic 4 Blocked Progress
Our protests N your
way? Think how we feel that we
have 2 protest this!
12/6/15
#pinkprivilege

Building v Talking *(4 "the activists")*
B clear. R U com-
plaining or constructing some-
thing better 4 us?
12/7/15

Misplaced Concern
They don't feel our pain
Incapable? Possibly
F*** em. Work on us
12/8/15

Ours 2 Start With
Don't ask 4 what is
our birthright. Take our sh** back
Demands must B made
12/9/15

Caustic Comfort
Can't understand what
we fear we're losing when we're
already losing
12/10/15

Artificially Flavored
(4 Oakland)
Gentrification
A way of replacing soul
with fabrication
12/11/15

Article 2, Section 1
Constitutional-
ly U've never voted 4
any president
12/12/15

Look At the Birdy
Stop giving these fools
your attention. These Rn't cam-
paigns. They're distractions
12/13/15

725,000psi - 2200°F
Possibly this pres-
sure is preparing us 2
love our freedom more
12/14/15

Not 2 B Taken 4 Granted
Resisters, remem-
ber 2 appreciate our
freedom when we win
12/15/15

Just A Little Further
I don't think we know
how close we R 2 triumph
Press 4ward full power
12/16/15

Planning 4 Success
This system will in-
evitably fall. Know what
we'll do when we win
12/17/15

"If U Don't Vote U Lose The Right 2 Complain???"
Vote? When has this coun-
try ever shown it's given
a sh** about U?
12/18/15
#f**kyall

The Good Ol' Boy Gangbang "Election" Time
A false choice of priv-
'leged men who wait N line 2
C who will fu** next
12/19/15

The Illusion of Choice
Vote: Choose from a pool
of fools your enemy gives
U 2 run your lives.
12/20/15

Sssssss
PCness kept rac-
ists repressed 4 far 2 long
They're exploding now
12/21/15

On The Tips of Their Tongues
They may not be say-
ing ni**a again YET but
actions speak louder
12/22/15

Recognize Your Worth
When it goes down KNOW
that we R capable. Don't
just switch oppressors
12/23/15

GoFundThem/'PressaGoGo

We R funding our
own oppression. Happy hol-
idays my people.
12/24/15

Working Fiction

Christmas, U.S. jus-
tice, Santa Klaus: Big profit
lies from the same source
12/25/15

Please Have Proof of Purchase

I'd like 2 return
these not guilty verdicts please
They R defective
12/26/15

& He Gave His Only Begotten Son 4 Your Sale
Thank God a Christ was
murdered 2 save U.S. re-
tail. Where's the wise men?
12/27/15

Ain't No Bystanders
A mother is shot
accidentally while mur-
dering a young boy
12/28/15

Give 'Em A Real Reason
They don't care because
we haven't made them care e-
nough to fear JustUs
12/29/15

Utter Disbelief/Y Am I Surprised?
How can 12 people
find the murder of a 12
year old justified?
12/30/15
#justiceforTamirRice

We Been Dun Toldju
When it happens, it's
on U. Should've been listening
a long time ago
12/31/15
#prophecy

January 2016

ChronoLIEgy
New Year's another
lie 2 control the mass thought
It's all dead. Change time.
1/1/15

A Little 2 4giving
Not amazed that we
made it another year. Shocked
at what we let slide
1/2/15

Not Enough Work
Not surprised that we
made it another year. Mad
we didn't change more
1/2/16

Blessed R the Agitators

Peace 2 the peace mak-
ers. The 1s that don't make peace
don't deserve any
1/3/15

After U Get Done Talking

2 many R fall-
ing while we sit making speech-
es & poems 4 change
1/4/15

Symbol-Banging Simian

U R an old toy
monkey manifesting be-
ing played N real life
1/5/15
#thatsnothiphop

1st Law of Apathy:
4 Every Non-Action There Is An Equal &
Opposite Lack of Action

1

Black genocide will
not end on election day
because of your vote
1/6/15

2

Murders by cops will
not end on election day
because of your vote
1/7/16

3

Mass imprisonment
continues on election
day despite your vote
1/8/16

U Must Not Know The Game
Ain't no lobbyists
putting up doe 2 end The
People's suffering
1/9/16

Teachable Moment
U.S. injustice
is profitable. Shows us
we're expendable
1/10/16

U're 2 Comfortable
Kept just complacent
enough 2 keep watching us
die. Get the fu** up!
1/11/16
#wakeup

N Line 4 Those New J's (*J is 4 Justice?*)
Fight 4 our justice
like U'll fight 4 new jumpers
the day they come out
1/12/16

N Line 4 Those New J's (*J is 4 Justice?*) 2
Fight 4 our justice
like U'll fight 4 ranchers' rights
2 land that's been stole
1/13/16

Shining Through
Bury our people
like our hidden histories
Our light still rises
1/14/16

Black Gold of the Sun
Even in this time
of darkness our brilliance bursts
through their suppression
1/15/16

Blind 2 Their Own Oppression
So much genera-
tional hate nurtured by few
2 suppress the rest
1/16/16

New Tactics Necessary
It's not hard 2 right
their injustice. Accept that
their way is not it.
1/17/16

I Quit
It's not hard 2 cor-
rect their evils. Our parti-
cipation must end
1/18/16

They Haven't Stopped, Baba Martin
They've killed thousands of
Kings B4 & after your
assassination
1/18/16
#MLK

Thank U, Baba Martin
Thank U 4 taking
the hits that we couldn't. Laid
ground 4 our work now.
1/18/16
#MLK

How Much Will U Take?
Not sure what we're wait-
ing 4. The call 2 change can't
B any louder
1/19/16

Something N the Water Does Not Compute
The State allowed it
The Feds know it & no 1's
been arrested yet
1/20/16
#rememberflint

#flintaintfixed

3rd World N America
Who knew Flint was a
3rd World country? Maybe just
its inhabitants?
1/21/16

Liquid Hate
Can they make their dis-
dain 4 our people any
more clear than N Flint?
1/22/16

Make It Happen People
Thank God The People
sent clean water 2 Flint. Their
gov didn't plan 2
1/23/16

Democracy At Work
US humani-
tarian work doesn't ap-
ply N its borders
1/24/16

#flintaintfixed #boycottnestle

Taste The Rainbow
Brown skins poisoned by
brown water tainted by dark
hearts greedy 4 green
1/25/16

Not N 'Merica
No such thing as po-
litical or corporate re-
sponsibility
1/26/16

...& Righteousness Like A Mighty Stream
After the water
drive these political crooks
out of their office
1/27/16

My Kinda Gal
If U ain't disrup-
ting like April Goggans, don't
call yourself gangsta
1/28/16

Politricks As Usual
Toupee's a ringer
Beware of what they're slipping
N behind this fool
1/29/16

...& 4 My Next Trick
Sleight of hand is the
name of the game N the pres-
idential campaign
1/30/16

The Answer Is Right N Front of U
Don't waste your time look-
ing 4 a savior when U've
got mirrors at home
1/31/16

February 2016

U Hear Me?
Moving forward, com-
munication will B our
most powerful tool
2/1/16

Say Something
Your silence doesn't
protect U. It covers our
offenders. Speak out.
2/2/16

Ya Mama's Calling (*re: 1948*)
Sons of Rosa Lee
Ingram, rise up & protect
your mother 2day
2/3/16
#RosaLeeIngram #protectBlackwomen

Ain't I A Woman? (*re: 1986*)
Most of my heroes
don't appear on no stamp but
Sojourner Truth did
2/4/16
#SojournerTruth

I'll Wait
R U expecting
justice from the same beings de-
stroying the planet?
2/5/16

The Ball's In Your Court
Don't hold athletes
& entertainers 2 task
Play your position
2/6/16

Beyhive (*re: Lemonade*)
With all this "slaying"
how about slaying self-hate
apathy & doubt
2/7/16

Beyhive 2
If it takes Beyon-
cé 2 wake U up, fine but
damn. Now get 2 work
2/8/16

Brilliantly Blind
The only thing more
brilliant than our beauty is
that we don't C it
2/9/16

Denial
The only thing strong-
er than our strength is our hes-
itance 2 use it
2/10/16

Let the Victims Pay
Y R the crimes of
criminal cops covered by
The People's taxes?
2/11/16

Skin In the Game... on the Blackhand side
My candidate would
have 2 run on the Black Pan-
ther Party ticket
2/12/16

The Illusion of Inclusion
(4 the LBJ revisionists)
2 insure a di-
vide Johnson made poor whites FEEL
better than rich blacks
2/13/16

Tasty Poisons
We are supposed to
trust a system that poisons
our food and water?
2/14/16

The Manufactured Fear & Irritation
I can't hide my skin
and I shouldn't ever feel
like there's a need to
2/15/16

U Might Have A Psychological Disorder
If truth offends U
accept that U R N love
with falsehoods & lies
2/16/16

U Should Probably C Someone
When U R offend
ed by truths it shows U'd rath-
er hide behind lies
2/17/16

Those Damn Pesky Victims
It's anti-police
sentiment 2 want their bru-
tality 2 stop?
2/18/16

Worth More Than Money
2day I've learned that
lies R this system's greatest
resource N the world
2/19/16

Circle the Wagons
If your 1st impulse
is 2 call the cops U've a-
greed 2 oppression
2/20/16

Brotha Malcolm
50+ years pass
it's still your lessons that res-
onate with me most
2/21/16

It Must B Nice
Priv'lege IS not hav-
ing 2 know the struggles of
others around U
2/22/16

Racism Affects Auditory Functions
Y do they hear hate
N the words of a people
fighting 4 their lives?
2/23/16

U May B A Bit 2 Patient
Change is not coming
fast enough because U R
not making it come
2/24/16

A Sucka Born Every Minute
I wanna thank Chump
4 making it clear how clue
less people can B
2/25/16

Acknowledge Yo Damn Self
Lesson: Bollywood
doesn't give a fu** about
winning an Oscar
2/26/16

Revolution Is A Parental Duty
Bringing children N
2 the world should B enough
2 fight 4 justice
2/27/16

Days Off?
Each day we don't fix
this world is another they
spend destroying it
2/28/16

Use Your Time Wisely
24 extra
hours 2 do some good where
some good could B done
2/29/16

March 2016

Old Habits – False Expectations
All your votes R 4
the same ol' system & U
really expect change?
3/1/16

Whatchu Gon' Do?
U ain't really that
mad. At least not mad enough
2 build 4 better
3/2/16

4 the Spectators
Really, it's fine if
U don't fight 4 justice. Stay
out of the way though
3/3/16

Real Bad Boys/Girls Move In Silence
Everybody's place
is not on the front line. Please
play your position
3/4/16

They Might've Missed the Memo
They say we're living
N the past as someone else
gets lynched on camera
3/5/16

U Mad We're Mad?
Can't get over a
past that's still VERY present
Revise your disdain
3/6/16

Chromatic
Why would they ever
paint me besides what I am
My shade must matter
3/7/16
#Kemet

Preparedness
Their hold is slipping
They're working a revision
plan. How about U?
3/8/16

Co-opt
Don't get sucked N by
"them," activists. Your mission
has yet 2 B done
3/9/16

Foreign Governments Have Been Toppled 4 Less
Don't think that if they'll
mark targets throughout the world
they won't do the hood???
3/10/16

"I Could've Saved Thousands More…"
U ain't got that "turn
back & get blasted" resolve
then U ain't ready
3/11/16
#MamaHarriet

Your Issue Is Not With Me
No 1's stealing A-
merican jobs. The corps R
giving them away
3/12/16
#capitalism #outsourcing

4 the Low Low
No 1's stealing A-
merican jobs. Slave wages
R just way cheaper
3/13/16

Vote 4 Me - I'll Set U Free!
So many distrac-
tions 2 hide the dirt the 1
% R doing
3/14/16

Ignorance Ain't Bliss
Knew your Elector-
al College rep B4 U
voted? Do U now?
3/15/16

Willfully Distracted
Y'all B missing the
easy truths 4 flashy lies
They won't hurt that bad
3/16/16

"Lightning Makes No Sound Until It Strikes"
Aleeyah said she
waited. Y'all didn't show up
so she handled it
3/17/16
#greatmomentsinBlackTwitterhistory
#AleeyahPorter

Real Bad Boys/Girls Move In Silence pt 2
Build it. Then tell us
it's built. They can't stop what has
already been done
3/18/16

I Hear U Talking?
Is your plan inclu-
sive of the People? The Peo-
ple sho' need a plan
3/19/16

Egoist Activist
Is your work 4 the
People or 4 U 2 B
the new 1%?
3/20/16

No New Massas
Replacing injus-
tice with more injustice is
no longer the way
3/21/16

Ain't Nuthin' 2 It...
We know that there is
a better way 2 do this
So please, let's do this
3/22/16

Room 4 Reevaluation 2morrow
Even if we're wrong
it'll B better than what
we're enduring now
3/23/16

When U work 2 correct a wrong, that wrong becomes a valuable lesson rather than a failure. Sometimes there's nothing wrong with being wrong. Admit it. Correct it. Learn from it but don't B scared 2 simply say, "I was wrong." That's where the growth begins.

Lock Frankenstein N with His Own Monster
Those who live off the
suffering of others should
have 2 live that way
3/24/16
#flintaintfixed #monsanto #bigpharm

Call 4 the producers, manufacturers, investors, engineers & heads of industry of the physical tools used 2 push the agenda in the pathology of European domination sit N a room with their families 4 48hrs breathing the sh** sprayed N those chemtrails, eating their alleged "farm-raised" chemical-laden meat & drinking red Kool-aid made from Flint MI's water. I think that's fair. That MIGHT look like justice.

Visualize This
U know what justice
looks like? Didn't think so. We
haven't seen it here.
3/25/16

Shot N Panavision
Justice should not be
a concept we only C
N movies 2day
3/26/16

B More Afraid That This BS Will Persist
Without Your Work
Let your Love 4 the
People outweigh the fear de-
signed 2 keep us down
3/27/16

Blindly Afraid
Fear's a mechanis-
m used 2 keep us from C'-
ing our enemy
3/28/16

Who Runs The World?!? FEAR.
Our common weakness
is fear. Our common ene-
my is who makes it
3/29/16

Who feeds the media the stories that keep U blind
& afraid? Who creates the monsters that R mur-
dering us N the streets? Who R those that ben-
efit from our own divisiveness, suffering & en-
gineered confusion? Keep asking questions until
U've got distinct faces on the culprits, then begin
2 bring them 2 justice. Part of their power is intan-
gibility. Demand their flesh. Extinguish the fear.

The Appetizer Recipe
Conceive a life full
of Love, without fear & we're
real close 2 winning
3/30/16

On Notice
U know they ain't sh**
Stare them N the face & let
them know they're g'on fall
3/31/16

April 2016

Somebody's Gonna B Reeeeeal Mad
When the truth comes out
pink folk will C they were pawns
& we were scapegoats
4/1/16

Dead Rationale
Voting 4 a less-
er evil is still the ac-
ceptance of evil
4/2/16

Lubricant?
Voting N Amer-
ica is a choice of how
U get fu**ed over
4/3/16

40%
How do U know how
far we can go when U've yet
2 put N that work
4/4/16

Values
What sense does it make
2 allow banks control of
your wealth AND your health?
4/5/16

Go 2 The Source
Bank's got your food, wa-
ter & shelter on lock. U
comfortable with that?
4/6/16

Maligned & Misaligned
Their agenda is
more wealth, less people. Ours is
2 live. U ready?
4/7/16

Mama Earth is Speaking
(Snow On A Spring Day)
2day is Sprinter
because we've allowed greed to
surpass common sense
4/8/16

Been There - Done That - Trying Something New
We've been resilient
It's time we start being more
Let's do triumphant!
4/9/16

Pull the Weeds
Break through the fear they
have planted & they R pow-
erless against us
4/10/16

C'mon People!
I believe N us
The US we can be against
all this tyranny
4/11/16

Can't Drink Your Kool-Aide
Beware enemies
that try 2 tell U who your
enemies should B
4/12/16

What is This? Organic or Something?
Between media
& food we've been fed fake so
long we can't C real
4/13/16

Hello??? I'm Standing Right Here!!!
When U don't control
your image they'll portray U
like U don't exist
4/14/16

#weseeyou

Who Left This Truck Here?
Guns N the hood would
not B a concern if pigs
stop supplying them
4/15/16

House Nigga
Black on Black crime is
sometimes done by boys N blue
What do U call that?
4/16/16

(Co) He Said, (Intel) She Said (Pro)
Instigation is
a dated trick that's never
gotten old 4 pigs
4/17/16

Step 1
The truth won't set us
free but it will point us N
the right direction
4/18/16

A Question of Genetics
Some of U R los-
ing your humanity. Some
lacked any 2 start
4/19/16

How 'Bout U Take A Swing At Injustice
Imagine if "World
Star" fights were focused N the
correct direction
4/20/16

"Don't Slice Your Nose 2 Spite Your Face"
Make "them" think it's a
Black issue. They'll serve
themselves up on a platter
4/21/16

Y R U Here!?!
Gentrification
is always heralded by lit-
tle dogs & their sh**
4/22/16

2 much Credit
We C them as hu-
man, failing 2 fathom the
depths of their evil
4/23/16

The Hypocritical Irony
After they've wrecked the
planet they want us 2 ur-
gently recycle
4/24/16

False Expectations
Where there is no con-
science or real consequence there
will B no justice
4/25/16

Sleeping Like Babies
No justice! No peace?
Didn't consider they rest
not giving a damn
4/26/16

Money Over Everything
(4 Dennis Hastert)
I've learned banking vi-
olations R worse than chi-
ld molestation
4/27/16

Membership Has Its Privileges
Structuring & fif-
teen months is what abuse costs
when U're N the club
4/28/16

Jesse'd
When "they" come 2 get
U it's usually the 1s
closest 2 U sent
4/29/16
#ripprince

Clouds On The Horizon
Killing our legends
will not stop your comeuppance
from happening soon
4/30/16
#1999

May 2016

"Quietly Endure, Silently Suffer and Patiently Wait"
They're comforted by
a lack of regret & years
of our inaction
5/1/16

Paying 4 Nature's Gifts
Organics: norma-
lizing paying 4 what's NOT
added 2 our food
5/2/16

Educated Dummies
Social disinte-
gration stems from being con-
ditioned not 2 think
5/3/16

In This Post-Racial Society
Where U R concerned
that your skin is a target
there is no justice
5/4/16

4 Cinco de Mayo
We celebrate the
small wins preparing 2 take
lead N the big ones
5/5/16

Inequality By Any Other Name
Where U R concerned
your gender is a target
there is no justice
5/6/16

Because We Have 2
We R masters of
compartmentalization
battling 4 peace
5/7/16

Isaiah 41:10
Move past the fear. It's
the only way that we've been
trapped all of these years
5/8/16

We R Capable
Move past the doubt. It's
the only thing that's held us
back 4 all these years
5/9/16

4 My Son
I raised him 2 B
a man N a world that strives
2 claim his manhood
5/10/16

Beast Mode (*4 Marshawn Lynch*)
We R unstoppa-
ble. Particularly when
we decide 2 B
5/11/16

The Prayer
Father-Mother, give
us clarity 2 C our
own frailties 2 fix
5/12/16

It's obvious that we R going 2 have 2 fix the is-
sues with the system we live N ourselves. How-
ever it is necessary 4 us 2 fix our issues within
ourselves 1st. Self, family, community, nation,
world. The healing begins at home.

Jason Had A Different Target (& *was fictional*)
Police brutali-
ty is way scarier than
Friday the 13th
5/13/16

#whywomendontreport

Ignorant Apathy & Indifference
Rape is only the
1st offense N a long line
of assaults some have
5/14/16

Rotten Muthafu**as
False accusations
R dangerous. Victim bla-
ming is just as bad
5/15/16

Aid & Abet
ANY rationa-
lization of rape makes U
a blind accomplice
5/16/16

Inbred Intellect

Rapists & racists
have the protection from i-
diots N common
5/17/16

The Source

Don't be mad at the
cake when it's the baker &
ingredients used
5/18/16

Thank U, Brotha Minister

Everyday that Mal-
colm's life impresses upon
mine I am grateful
5/19/16

Apples & Oranges

There is a diffe-
rence between what is called law
& what is justice
5/20/16

Uniformed Turncoat
Killing your country-
men 4 work N your country
makes U a traitor
5/21/16

In The Past?
How do U 4give
an offender that's never
stopped their offenses?
5/22/16

Da Hell is Wrong With Hillary?
How do we get pass
a brutal past that's never
passed N2 the past?
5/23/16

Matthew 5:5

Have the audaci-
ty 2 make change. The meek may
not B here 4 it
5/24/16

Scripture has kept a many a (wo)man enslaved

Don't B bound by re-
ligion. We R the saviors
we seek. Act like it.
5/24/16

Cannibals

Justice is blocked by
thousands of buzz cut sheep well
trained 2 act like wolves
5/25/16

It Ain't Over, Muthafu**as
Their "fu** U" 2 Flint's
water's a fu** U 2 the
People everywhere
5/26/16
#rememberflint

I Pledge Allegiance… 2 Whom???
A lot of jigs be-
lieve N a cotton uni-
form over their skin
5/27/16

2 Brotha/Sista Black & Blue
Dear Officer Lost
Your job is not more impor-
tant than your people
5/28/16

Cognitive Dissonance
These cowards have con-
vinced themselves they do what they
do 2 keep us safe
5/29/16

A Memorial Day Musing
Credit 4 what en-
slaved people have done has gone
on 4 far 2 long
5/30/16

U're Getting Sleepy. Sleeeepy…
So I heard they re-
made Roots 2 make U think U
weren't already here
5/31/16

June 2016

Stand On It
Know our greatness through
study & don't fight fools o-
ver what U have learned
6/1/16

Enrich – Uplift – Elevate
Defend our greatness
through action by making those
around U greater
6/2/16

Our Mission
We have a commu-
nity 2 defend & a
damaged world 2 heal
6/3/16

The G.O.A.T.
Ali showed the world
more than mere greatness. He showed
us integrity
6/4/16
#muhammadali

The Stewards
We have a commu-
nity 2 rebuild & a
hurt world 2 reclaim
6/5/16

Involved Either 1 Way or the Other
U're either commit-
ted 2 our salvation or
2 our destruction
6/6/16

#notmypresident

Keep Your Eye On the Birdie
Y'all R really fall-
ing 4 this Chump sh**? Please watch
4 the sleight of hand
6/7/16

U Can't B This Gullible
The same ones saying
Prince died of drugs R the same
ones covering Chump
6/8/16

Cathartic Pain
Everyday I write
the sadness grows. I'm writing
2 kill the sadness

Afterworks

#KorrynGaines #sayhername

Happy Slaves
Negroes will justi-
fy their own murders until
they themselves R dead
8/3/16

House Ni**as
Nobody justi-
fies their own oppression like
negroes on camera
8/3/16

Weak Links N the Chain
Korryn stood on her
square. Where were those who should have
been standing with her?
8/3/16

Move Free
Free Black expression
looks crazy on plantations
full of happy slaves
8/6/17
insp. by Kizzy & Sam Greenlee

Obama
Brown imperial-
ism is not a shade bet-
ter than the pink kind
4/3/18

On The Plantation of Commercial Music
Feeling invisi-
ble 4 years, niggas R thirs-
ty 4 attention
1/18/19
#thatsnothiphop

As A Result
Feeling invisi-
ble 4 years, ni**as is dy-
ing 4 attention
1/19/19
#victimsoftheirownignorance

Damned if U do
Surrendering 2
savages only gets U
shot in the armpits
1/21/19

The Many Faces of American Politics
Y B the face of
those who rule when U can sim-
ply B the ruler
4/5/19
#Chicago #mayoralelection

Soul Crushing Weight
A ni**a is what
is created when Blacks fold
under "the Pressure"
4/10/19

They Smile In Your Face...
Beware enemies
who try 2 tell U who your
enemies should B
4/12/19

Go Away Already
I am bored with "Eu
ro supremacy." When's the
expiration date?
4/17/19

N Remembrance Of U

I write these haiku
2 resurrect what they would
rather we 4get
6/5/19

There's Power N Our Joy

Your happiness is
an act of revolution
Fight 4 it fiercely
6/18/19

All Of The Earth & Ancestors R Waiting

ALL this BS ends
when we decide 2 end it
It's time we end this
7/4/19
#independenceday

Thanks 4 reading